P9-DXK-904

WONDERS
OF THE **WORLD**

Mummies

Other books in the Wonders of the World series include:

Gems
Geysers
Icebergs
Quicksand

WONDERS
OF THE **WORLD**

Mummies

Stuart A. Kallen

**KIDHAVEN
PRESS**™

THOMSON

GALE

San Diego • Detroit • New York • San Francisco • Cleveland
New Haven, Conn. • Waterville, Maine • London • Munich

© 2003 by KidHaven Press. KidHaven Press is an imprint of The Gale Group, Inc., a division of Thomson Learning, Inc.

KidHaven™ and Thomson Learning™ are trademarks used herein under license.

For more information, contact
KidHaven Press
27500 Drake Rd.
Farmington Hills, MI 48331-3535
Or you can visit our Internet site at http://www.gale.com

LIBRARY OF CONGRESS CATALOGING-IN-PUBLICATION DATA

Kallen, Stuart A., 1955–
    Mummies / by Stuart A. Kallen.
        p. cm. — (Wonders of the world)
Includes bibliographical references and index.
    ISBN 0-7377-1031-4 (hardback : alk. paper)
Summary: Discusses the golden age of Egyptian mummies, mummification, the embalming and wrapping process, and significant mummy discoveries and locations.
    1. Mummies—Juvenile literature. [1. Mummies.] I. Kallen, Stuart A., 1955– II. Title.
    GN293 .B64 2003
    393'.3—dc21

2002005388

Printed in the United States of America

CONTENTS

The Golden Age of Mummies

Mummies have fascinated and frightened people for thousands of centuries. As dead bodies that have been preserved, mummies connect the modern world to ancient history. And they serve as a reminder that people's physical appearance has changed little since ancient times. But their hollow eyes and blank faces remain spooky and unsettling.

Mummies are the dried remains of human or animal bodies that have been prevented from decaying naturally. Some of these dead bodies may have been mummified accidentally by natural conditions such as freezing under an icy glacier, or lying under a thick, airless bog. But the most famous mummies were made thousands of years ago by the ancient Egyptians, who built an advanced society—including the great pyramids

The ancient Egyptians constructed some of the most mysterious of all ancient monuments like the sphinx, which stands guard over the pyramids at Giza.

and wondrous temples and monuments—on the banks of the Nile River.

The golden age of Egyptian mummies began more than five thousand years ago, around 3400 B.C. and lasted until 600 B.C. During this time, the Egyptians preserved, or **embalmed**, their dead for religious reasons. They believed that the spirit, or soul, left the body when a person died, but returned after a short time. For the soul to live forever, it needed the body to remain intact. As a result, the Egyptians perfected a system using special chemicals to mummify bodies for the afterlife. But preserving a **corpse** was a complex, expensive, and time-consuming process. As a result, the service was performed mainly for rich people. And it was also done for animals that were considered sacred, including cats, birds, dogs, and even crocodiles.

Removing the Organs

When a wealthy Egyptian died, the relatives ordered their servants to deliver the body to the embalming workshop, called the *wabt*. There they were met by priests who were waiting with their embalming tools.

The priests had to move quickly, because a dead body begins to putrefy, or rot, almost immediately. The men laid the corpse out on a special table and two events happened: The priests conducted a religious ceremony while, at the same time, embalming the body.

The ceremony was led by a chief priest who wore a jackal mask representing **Anubis**, the Egyptian god of mummification. A second priest carefully washed the

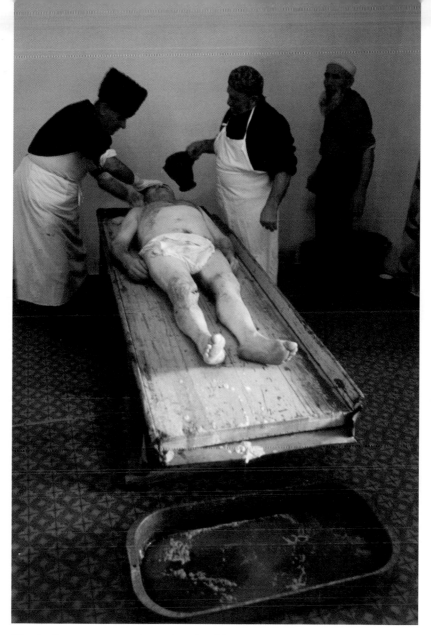

Embalmers prepare a body. The process of embalming bodies began with the work of the ancient Egyptians.

body while a third chanted prayers and magic spells. Another priest, known as the scribe, drew a mark along the left side of the body where an incision was made. Another priest then picked up his ceremonial **flint** knife

Alaska

Canada

Denmark

England

Italy

Rome Greece

Arizona

Egypt

Mexico

New Guinea

Peru

Chile

▲ mummies discovered in these locations

Mummy Discoveries Around the World

and ripped a cut down the left side of the body. Next, the intestines, liver, lungs, stomach, and other internal organs were removed. The organs were carefully stored in special clay containers, called **canopic jars**. Because the Egyptians believed that the heart governed intelligence, this organ was left in the body.

To remove the brain, the priests pushed a thin bronze wire, similar to a hooked knitting needle, up the corpse's nose and pulled it out piece by piece. This material was simply thrown away because the Egyptians did not realize that the brain was an important organ that controlled all bodily functions.

Then, the body cavity was carefully washed and rinsed with spices and palm wine. This was probably done in an effort to disguise the horrible smell that was emanating from the body.

Drying the Body

After the organs were removed, the priests needed to completely **dehydrate** the body. They also had to kill any bacteria that would cause the mummy to putrefy. This process was performed using a natural salt, call **natron**, that was found along the banks of Egyptian lakes.

Natron was heaped upon the cadaver and left for a period of forty days. During this time, the salt leached all moisture from the body. When the process was finished, the corpse was shriveled and black but dry and elastic.

Great care was given to the mummy to plump it out, that is, return it to its natural shape. Priests first filled the body cavity with sand, sawdust, or linen rags soaked in pine resin. Clumps of linen were also pushed into the cranium, the area of the skull where the brain had been removed. When this process was finished, the wound on the left side of the body was stitched closed. Then, to prevent the skin from cracking, the entire body was rubbed with a special lotion made from a combination of beeswax, juniper oil, spices, and natron.

The nose was plugged with more linen. Rags were also pushed into the mouth so that the cheeks would not look sunken. Pads were put into the eye sockets and the eyelids were pulled shut. In later years, artificial wooden eyeballs painted to look like real eyes were pushed into

Mummification included wrapping the body in linen gauze and placing a death mask on the face of the deceased.

the eye sockets. Finally, the plumped body was covered with a molten (liquid) resin from head to toe.

Wrapping the Mummy

While great care was given to the mummy's appearance, the body would be seen by only the gods because the next step covered the corpse completely.

To finish the work, the chief priest wrapped hundreds of feet of linen bandages around the entire corpse. He started with each finger and worked his way down to the legs and feet. Between layers, the bandages were coated with a sticky pine resin so they would remain waterproof. Small magic objects, called amulets, were placed between the layers of linen. Prayers were chanted the entire time. This lengthy process took about fifteen days to complete.

When the wrapping was finished, a red burial shroud was wrapped tightly around the body. So that the gods would recognize the face of the dead, a lifelike mask was placed over the head.

The Funeral

By then, seventy days had passed since the person had died, and his or her mummified body was ready for the funeral. During this event, solemn religious ceremonies, which were as important as the mummification process, were conducted.

During the funeral, the body was placed in a coffin and sent down the Nile River in a boat to the cemetery. The boat was packed with professional mourners hired

After last rites had been performed, the mummy was laid
in a sarcophagus and sealed within a tomb.

by the family. The mourners wept and wailed as loudly as possible so that people standing along the river banks could not fail to notice the funeral.

Once the procession reached the tomb, a ceremony called the Opening of the Mouth was performed so that the mummy would be able to use its senses to eat, drink, see, and smell in the afterlife. Finally, the mummy was placed in a tomb which was then sealed, and the work of more than ten weeks was finished.

Other Mummies

The Egyptians were not the only people to mummify their dead. The Greeks, who adopted some Egyptian customs, made their own mummies around A.D. 300. The Roman culture, modeled after the Greeks, also mummified corpses. In South America, native tribes in the Andes Mountains of Peru practiced the custom by smoke-drying their dead. And mummies have been found in many parts of North America including Arizona and Alaska. Wherever ancient cultures wanted to preserve their dead, people have perfected the art of mummification to keep their corpses for eternity.

King Tut and His Amazing Tomb

King Tutankhamen, or King Tut, was born more than thirty-three hundred years ago in 1333 B.C. He became king, or pharaoh, when he was only nine years old and died at the age of eighteen. Although he was not an important king, he is well known today because his tomb was the richest royal burial chamber ever found.

King Tut ruled during a period in Egypt of power and wealth. As a result, pharaohs were buried with great treasures. These tombs, however, attracted grave robbers. Around 1000 B.C., in order to foil thieves, all the surviving royal mummies in Egypt were gathered together and buried in two secret hiding places cut in the remote Valley of the Kings in Thebes. This area was so barren and isolated that the mummies and their royal treasures lay undiscovered for more than thirty-three centuries.

Amazing Discoveries

In November 1922, British archaeologist Howard Carter—who had been searching the Valley of the Kings for five years—discovered a buried stairway that descended into the desert floor. After workmen unearthed twelve steps, Carter found a heavy door. Instead of entering the passage, however, he ordered his workmen to rebury it. After posting guards at the site, Carter sent for a wealthy Englishman, Lord Carnarvon, who had been financing Carter's explorations for five years.

When Carnarvon arrived about two weeks later, the men finally drilled through the door. They found themselves in a long hallway that led to a second door that opened into a room, called an antechamber. What they saw there astounded them. The room was filled with a treasure trove of more than three thousand ancient objects fit for a king.

There was a dizzying array of furniture including three couches carved into animal shapes. They also found chests, mirrors, chairs, and stools. Stacked around the room like a cluttered

The golden sarcophagus of King Tutankhamen displays the beautiful craftsmanship of ancient artisans.

From left to right, Howard Carter, Lord Carnarvon, and an assistant carefully inspect treasures found in King Tut's tomb.

basement, the men found a chariot in pieces, 130 walking sticks, and sporting equipment including 46 bows, 400 arrows, clubs, boomerangs, and knives.

Trunks contained clothing such as sandals, necklaces, linen loincloths, slippers decorated with gold, and embroidered gloves. So that the tomb's resident would not be hungry in the afterlife, the antechamber contained baskets of watermelon seeds and large jars of vintage wine. No one had touched these items in nearly thirty-three hundred years. This was the greatest treasure trove ever discovered in Egypt.

The men hoped that this was the legendary tomb of King Tutankhamen, and a door in the antechamber beckoned to the archaeologists. But they decided to carefully explore the antechamber before pushing on.

Carter assembled a team of respected archaeologists to catalog the find. Each object was photographed,

Tut's tomb yielded thousands of treasures from the ancient world, such as this gilded jewelry box.

WONDERS OF THE WORLD • **MUMMIES**

loaded on to a padded stretcher, and removed from the tomb. Items were then cleaned, repaired, and shipped to the Cairo Museum. After seven weeks, the job of clearing the antechamber was finished.

Finally Finding Tut

Finally, plans were made to open the last room—the burial chamber—which was guarded by two life-sized statues of Egyptian soldiers, called sentinels. As dozens of people watched, Carter pounded a hole in the door. Finally, he pushed a candle through the door. In the dim wavering light, Carter saw an astounding wall of what appeared to be solid gold. Upon further examination, the wall turned out to be part of a huge gold-plated shrine that nearly filled the room.

Inside the shrine were three more shrines. After carefully removing these objects, Carter found a stone coffin, called a **sarcophagus**. Inside this object were three more coffins, each tightly laid inside the next. The last coffin was six feet long and weighed 222 pounds. And it was made of solid gold! This priceless coffin contained the mummified body of King Tutankhamen.

The process of removing the shrines and coffins from the burial chamber was very time consuming. The shrines needed to be taken apart piece by piece, and the coffins were heavy and difficult to maneuver.

The Mummy's Curse

Meanwhile, the Egyptian workers who did most of the work were afraid that disturbing the tomb might bring the

When Carter entered the king's burial chamber, he removed the lid of this stone sarcophagus. Egyptian workers at the site feared that disturbing the tomb might unleash a curse on them.

curse of the pharaoh upon them. This fear was heightened in February 1923 when Lord Carnarvon developed a high fever. Doctors believed that he fell ill from a mosquito bite on the cheek that became infected when nicked by a razor while shaving. But the local people believed that the Englishman had received the mummy's curse. And before long, Carnarvon himself came to believe it.

Although the fever finally went away, it returned again, finally killing Carnarvon two months later on April 5. Rumors of King Tut's curse continued to spread after Carnarvon's death was marked by several unusual events. At the exact moment he died, the electric power in Cairo failed and the lights stayed out for several hours. No one could ever explain why this happened.

Also, back in England at the moment of Carnarvon's death, his dog Suzie let out a loud, piercing howl and died instantly. Again, there was no explanation, but the newspapers found out about the event and blamed it on the mummy's curse.

Other Mysterious Deaths

Carnarvon's passing may have been considered a coincidence if he were the only one to die. But several weeks later, a wealthy American executive, George Jay Gould, died of a high fever within days of touring Tut's tomb. Another rich American, Joel Wool, also died of a fever after a visit to the burial chamber.

While Wool, Gould, and Carnarvon were all in poor health before their visits, archaeologist Arthur Cruttenden was in fine health when he helped Carter open Tut's burial chamber in 1922. Cruttenden, however, became ill at that time and died in 1928.

By 1929 at least thirteen people who had visited Tut's grave died suddenly. Another thirteen who were associated with the excavation, including Carnarvon's brother, also died mysteriously. Others experienced long illnesses marked by fatigue and fever.

A Possible Answer

In the 1930s the public's fascination with the mummy's curse continued to grow. And filmmakers in Hollywood saw a golden opportunity to take advantage of the mummy craze. The first horror movie dealing with the subject was the 1932 film *The Mummy*, about a thirty-seven-hundred-year-old mummy brought back to life after its tomb is unearthed by archaeologists.

A series of movies in the 1940s were titled *The Mummy's Hand*, *The Mummy's Curse*, *The Mummy's Ghost*, and *The Mummy's Tomb*. The 1950s saw the silly comedy *Abbott and Costello Meet the Mummy*. And movie mummies made a big comeback in recent times with 1997's *Bram Stoker's The Mummy*, 1999's *The Mummy*, and 2001's *The Mummy Returns*.

While tall tales of horrible mummies continue to sell, scientists now blame toxic mold for the deaths of

The 1999 film *The Mummy* demonstrates that public fascination with mummies has endured well into the modern age.

those who toured Tutankhamen's burial chamber. And the ancient king himself was in pretty bad shape when he was finally unwrapped. Despite the intricate shrines and coffins built to protect him over the centuries, his body was badly decayed when Carter removed the bandages. While his mummified corpse was hidden from robbers for more than thirty-three hundred years, it proved impossible to protect him against the relentless hand of time.

Bog Bodies

While many ancient cultures went to great lengths to preserve the dead, some mummies are created by accidents of nature.

Marshy wetlands known as **bogs** produce the perfect environment for mummification. These natural areas of moist, soggy ground are formed when reeds, moss, and other waterlogged plants fill in a watery pool.

Unlike water in lakes, rivers, and other wetlands, bog water contains very little oxygen, because it is very still, or stagnant. Without air, bogs cannot support bacteria and other microscopic organisms that help dead plants and animals rot and decay. And the plants that do live in bogs contain high levels of acid, which is released in the water when they die. As a result, bog water is as acidic as the vinegar in a jar of pickles. And it preserves organisms just as well.

In addition, sphagnum moss, or peat moss, one of the few plants that thrive in bogs, contains **tannin**. This substance has long been used to tan and preserve leather and other animal hides.

When bogs combine tannin and vinegar-like water to pickle organisms, but little air to support bacteria, they become nature's perfect preserver of the dead.

Pulled from the Bogs

Although bogs are harsh environments that support little life, they are also a rich natural resource. The peat that is formed there is cut by workers, who then dry it in the sun. Peat logs are then burned in special stoves used for cooking and heating homes. In Europe and Great Britain, people have been cutting peat for centuries, and mummified remains of hundreds of men, women, and children have been pulled from the bogs by workers.

"Bog bodies" come in all forms. Some are complete bodies while others are just hands, feet, or even heads. A few of the mummies are well preserved, while others are merely skeletons with small amounts of hair and skin. Because of the tannin in the water, bog bodies take on a distinctive dark brown color. And they range in age from almost ten thousand years old to several hundred years old.

When bog bodies are found, there is usually speculation as to how they ended up there. Some seem to have been unlucky people who simply fell in the muck and drowned. Others appear to be human sacrifices of-

Bogs have served as the dumping grounds for bodies over thousands of years.

fered up by primitive cultures that were celebrating a military victory or hoping to appeal to the gods. Other bog bodies are murder victims who were tossed away by killers hoping to hide their deadly crime. Whatever the motive, many bog bodies show obvious signs of violence, such as ax cuts, stab wounds, bashed skulls, and slashed throats.

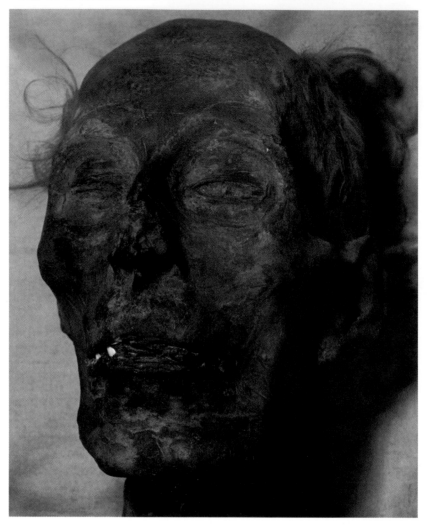

Bog bodies can be distinguished by the dark pallor of their skin, a quality given to them by the tannin in bog water.

Danish Bog Queen

One mummy that met a brutal end is the Haraldskaer woman, found on the Haraldskaer estate in Denmark in 1835. When the woman was discovered by peat cutters, her gross and twisted body had been blackened but amazingly preserved by the bog.

When the find was reported, some scholars believed the mummy was the body of the ancient Norse queen Gunhild. According to a folk legend, Gunhild was drowned in the bog on the orders of a Danish king called Blue Tooth.

After the mummy was found, nineteenth-century Danish king Frederick VI had a beautiful wooden coffin carved for her. The woman thought to be Queen Gunhild was laid to rest in a stone mausoleum in a church cemetery in Vejle.

For more than one hundred years, controversy simmered over the entombed mummy, with some researchers stating that she had died centuries before Queen Gunhild was born. Finally in 1977, archaeologist J.J.A. Worsaae tested the mummy using a scientific method called radiocarbon dating, a test that can accurately reveal the age of an object. Worsaae determined that the mummy was born some fifteen hundred years before the queen, and he guessed that the mummy was a victim of an ancient sacrifice. Despite this proof, the mummy queen remains in the church cemetery next to more recently deceased Danish kings and queens.

Huldre Fen Mummy

Another female bog body found in Denmark might have actually been an ancient queen—or at least a rich person. This mummy was found about one hundred years ago in a bog named Huldre Fen. The woman, who died around A.D. 95, was found wearing a head scarf, a sheepskin cape, and a checkered shirt. She also possessed a finely carved comb made from deer horn, and a few amber beads. Because most bog bodies are found naked, researchers believe that this woman must have held a high place in society to have been laid to rest in such a manner.

The Grauballe Man's Last Meal

In 1952 another Danish mummy in very good condition was pulled from the bog at Grauballe. The body of the Grauballe man, believed to have died around 55 B.C., was unusually well preserved, except for his bones, which had dissolved. The skin of the Grauballe man was black, leathery, firm, and supple. The internal organs were undamaged, and even his fingerprints were intact. There was no mystery as to the mummy's cause of death, however. His neck was slit from ear to ear, leaving little doubt the Grauballe man was murdered.

This Danish mummy is remarkably preserved, down to the finest detail.

A man displays the mummy of a tribal chief found in New Guinea.

Because his stomach was in good shape, scientists were able to determine what the man had for his last meal. Researchers found remains of vegetable barley soup and a sort of granola made from the seeds of more than sixty different plants. Scientists concluded that the Grauballe man was a tall, dark-haired man in his late thirties, killed in the winter by a blow to the head. He was then stripped of his clothing and possessions, his throat was cut, and he was thrown into the bog.

The Lindow Man

A mummy found in Lindow Moss, a bog in Cheshire, England, also revealed the man's last meal. But the Lindow man was discovered in pieces over time, and his body has been reassembled throughout the years.

In 1984 peat cutters found the head, torso, and right foot of the Lindow man. Then in 1988 they came upon his skin, left leg, right thigh, and other body parts. Researchers put the pieces together and determined that the Lindow man died between A.D. 2 and 119.

Like earlier finds, several theories were put forth about the mummy. His beard, hair, and nails were neatly trimmed, showing him to be a tribal chief or a wealthy man. There is little doubt he met a violent end, however. Some speculate that his body was in pieces because he was chopped up and sacrificed. Wounds show that he might have been savagely murdered by strangling, stabbing, or beating with the flat side of an ax. At least the man did not die hungry. His stomach contained a bread-like cake made from grains and pollen.

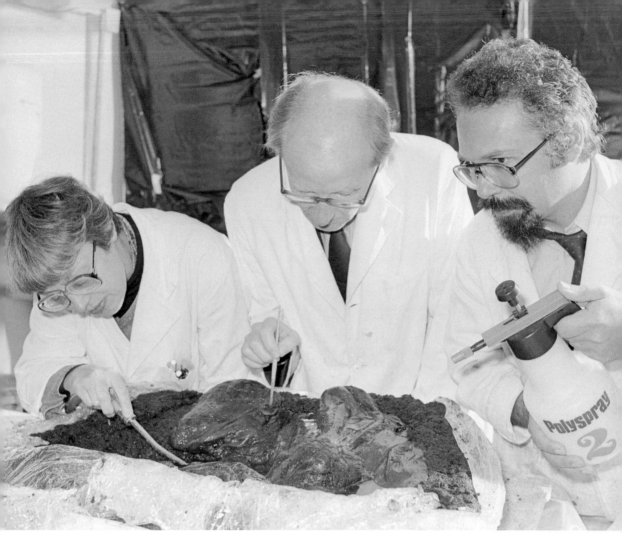

Scientists work to clean and reassemble the Lindow man.

Gruesome Deaths

Every bog body discovered is unique. The mummies have been young, old, and middle aged. But most experienced extremely gruesome deaths. They may have been crime victims or sacrificed to long-forgotten gods and goddesses. Whatever the case, when the bogs give up their dead, they reveal tantalizing details that open a window to the past.

Otzi the Iceman

As anyone with a refrigerator knows, frozen food will remain fresh for a long time because ice and freezing temperatures have a powerful preservation effect. Although rare, human bodies may also become mummified by freezing. The Iceman, a mummy found in the early 1990s in Italy, is one of those ancient mysteries frozen in time. And he has revealed more about the past than almost any mummy since King Tut.

On September 19, 1991, two German mountain climbers were hiking near the Italian-Austrian border in the Tyrolean Alps more than ten thousand feet above sea level. While trekking across a snowfield, they found a frozen body partially encased in the ice of a glacier. (Glaciers are large sheets of ice found in mountain areas that are formed over many centuries and do not usually

Scientists search the site where the body of the Iceman was recovered.

melt in the summer. This glacier, however, had melted because of unusual weather conditions.)

The hikers called the police, thinking they had found the body of a lost hiker or a murder victim. When news of the discovery was brought to the public's attention, about a dozen public officials and curious hikers climbed up to the Iceman's grave.

Chipping Away the Ice

At that time, people had no idea of the importance of this discovery. Hoping to quickly free the corpse, they carelessly hacked away at the surrounding ice with ski poles and ice axes. When those did not work, they picked up what they thought were sticks and began to hit the ice with those, breaking them. In reality, these sticks were wooden pieces of the Iceman's backpack and hunting bow—priceless treasures of the distant past. And as the curious crowd yanked on the Iceman's body to pull him from the ice, they shredded his ancient clothing. Police later arrived with a jackhammer. While chipping away the ice, they accidentally hit the body with the powerful tool, leaving a large nick in the hip.

Once the body was airlifted to Innsbruck, Austria, a horde of photographers crowded into the morgue to snap pictures of the local curiosity. The heat from the flashbulbs caused a fungus to grow on the mummy, further damaging it. Meanwhile, medical examiners determined that the leathery skinned body was not a lost hiker, but that of a mummy. Still, they assumed the corpse was only several hundred years old.

Otzi: The Oldest

Finally, on September 24, five days after the discovery, a local archaeologist, Professor Konrad Spindler, examined the body. After determining the age of some tools found alongside the Iceman, the professor excitedly announced that the mummy was at least four thousand years old. This ranked the Iceman as one of the oldest and best-preserved mummies ever discovered. (By way of comparison, King Tut is about thirty-three hundred years old.) And the Iceman was by far the oldest body ever found in a glacier, predating his nearest competitor by thirty-six hundred years.

The professor took immediate steps to preserve the mummy, placing it in a freezer at twenty-one degrees with 98 percent humidity—the exact same temperature that had kept the Iceman intact for forty centuries.

Preserved by Luck

The Iceman was quickly nicknamed Otzi for the Otztal Valley, the area in which he was discovered. And like King Tut in the 1920s, Otzi quickly became a worldwide star. Hundreds of stories were written about him in the press. Meanwhile, local vendors sold postcards, coffee

Dr. Konrad Spindler closely examines the well-preserved body and tools of Otzi the Iceman.

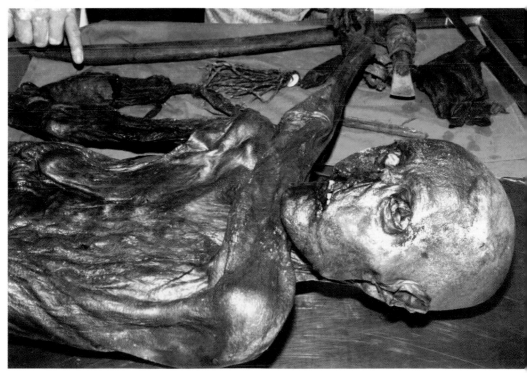

mugs, posters, and T-shirts with Otzi's image. He even had a hit song written about him in Austria.

As scientists continued to examine the Iceman, they realized that he had survived throughout the centuries by sheer luck. It seems that he died in a hollowed-out place in the rocks that soon filled in with snow. Usually the movement of glaciers crushes and tears anything trapped underneath. But the snow over Otzi's grave acted as a cushion to protect his body from destruction by the ice sheet. As a result, the Iceman was naturally mummified when the ice-cold temperatures leached all of the moisture from his body. In fact, his body was in such good condition that even his eyeballs were preserved, eerily gazing from the distant past at his modern-day rescuers.

The Iceman had small, black burnlike stripe marks on his lower back, behind his knee, and on his ankle. These marks were tattoos, probably made by soot from charcoal being forced under cuts in the skin. The tattoos were thought to be magical markings meant to protect him, or even ease the pain of the joints where they were placed.

The Iceman's Tools

Scientists continued to study the corpse, and they ran a radiocarbon test on the body. This showed that Otzi lived between 3500 and 3000 B.C., making him between five thousand and fifty-five hundred years old, at least a millennium older than Professor Spindler had guessed.

Otzi was born during the Copper Age, which lasted in Europe from about 4000 to 2200 B.C. During this time, people dug exposed veins of copper from mountains, such

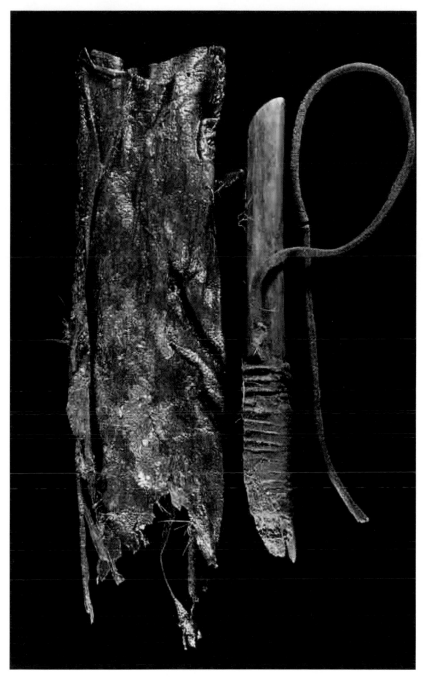

The Iceman carried a variety of survival tools, including an ax with a pure copper head, a dagger made of flint and wood, and a bone needle for sewing garments.

Otzi the Iceman was discovered in the Tyrolean Alps.

as the Alps, and melted the soft metal in very hot fires. The liquid metal was poured into molds for shaping into weapons, tools, and utensils.

During his travels in the Alps, the Iceman carried an ax with a pure copper head. It was attached to a wooden handle with birch sap gum and tightly wrapped with a rawhide rope. He carried other survival tools as well, including a small ash wood-handled flint dagger, a bone needle for repairing clothes, some grass rope, and flint used to start fires.

The Iceman also carried twelve unfinished arrows with flint heads and an unfinished bow about six feet in length. (This was repaired after rescuers broke it while digging his body from the ice). The arrows were kept in a well-crafted pouch made of deer skin.

The Iceman's Last Days

Intense study of the Iceman's tools revealed facts about the last day of his life. By looking at the items under powerful microscopes, scientists found bits of animal hair, blood, and tissue on the knife and ax. It is believed that Otzi killed an animal and butchered the meat with his blades.

After his last meal, Otzi the Iceman might have climbed into the mountains to find some flint to finish his arrows. After night fell, he went to sleep. The temperature dropped rapidly, possibly from a storm, and

Scientists examine the remains of Otzi the Iceman in a freezer where temperatures prevent him from decaying.

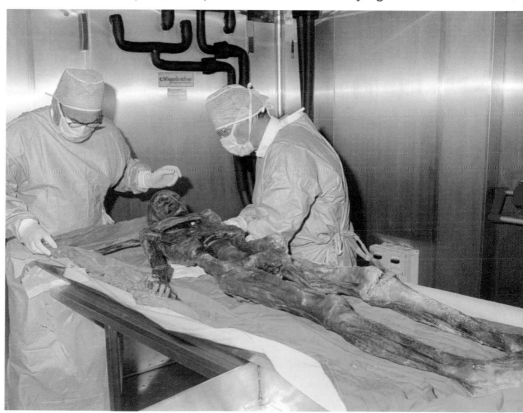

41

Otzi froze to death, only to lie undiscovered for more than five millennia.

While Otzi's death was probably a mystery to his surviving family, he has yielded a wealth of knowledge about life in the distant past. And modern people remain fascinated with the Iceman. Since his body was put in display in the South Tyrol Museum of Archaeology in 1998, more than a quarter million people have walked past his mummified corpse, to look into his eyes and see a preserved relic of their distant relative who once roamed the Tyrolean Alps during a long-ago period known as the Copper Age.

Glossary

Anubis: The Egyptian god of mummification.

bog: Areas of spongy, waterlogged ground where sphagnum moss and peat are found.

canopic jars: Clay vessels where the internal organs of the dead were stored during Egyptian mummification ceremonies.

corpse: A dead body.

dehydrate: To preserve by removing water.

embalm: To treat (a corpse) with preservatives in order to prevent decay.

flint: A very hard stone that makes sparks when struck, and is used to start fires.

natron: A natural salt found along the banks of desert lakes that was used for dehydrating bodies.

sarcophagus: A stone coffin, often decorated with words or artwork.

tannin: Plant-based chemicals used for preserving animal skins.

wabt: A building used by ancient Egyptians, where the processes of embalming and mummification were conducted.

For Further Exploration

Janet Buell, *Bog Bodies*. New York: Twenty-First Century Books, 1997. Detailed stories about mummies pulled from bogs in England and other parts of Europe.

Nathaniel Harris, *Mummies*. New York: Franklin Watts, 1995. A book about mummies of the world including those from Egypt, Greenland, Denmark, and elsewhere.

Dorothy Hinshaw Patent, *Secrets of the Ice Man*. New York: Benchmark Books, 1999. The complete story of Otzi the Iceman, found in the Italian Alps in 1991.

James Putnam, *Mummy*. New York: Alfred A. Knopf, 1993. A book with many colorful pictures and interesting facts about mummies from around the world.

Index

Picture Credits

About the Author

Stuart A. Kallen is the author of more than 150 nonfiction books for children and young adults. He has written on topics ranging from the theory of relativity to rock and roll history to life on the American frontier. In addition, Mr. Kallen has written award-winning children's videos and television scripts. In his spare time, the author is a singer/songwriter/guitarist living in San Diego, California.